10 SECONDS TO CHILD GENIUS

-

The Road to Child Genius™ Part 2

Tips and advice on becoming a Child Genius on television

TRAY-SEAN BEN SALMI
AKA
CHILD GENIUS ADVISOR
AMAZON #1 BEST SELLER, AWARD WINNING AUTHOR
AS SEEN ON RADIO & TELEVISION

Published by Influencer Publishing in 2019

Copyright © Tray-Sean Ben Salmi 2019

Second Edition

The author asserts the moral right under the Copyright, Designs and Patents Act 1988 to be identified as the author of this work.

ISBN: 978-1-913310-12-7

'YOU' called this book to you because you live in every changing world and you want to be a part of that change. Everything starts with an idea or concept in your mind. The idea or concept is given form by taking action and manifesting your **dream**s. Then the magic begins to happen during the construction process. That process begins here and **now**!

This book is dedicated to children and youth everywhere...

Cover Design by Swiss Graphics

3

ACKNOWLEDGEMENTS

We would like to thank the universe for all wealth, health, happiness, opportunities, abundance and support that we have received and experienced! We would also like to take this opportunity to thank all the amazing people that have supported us guided us and taught us along our journey. We really and truly would not be where we are today if it was not for family friends and partners.

We would also like to take this opportunity to acknowledge those of you who have delivered adversity to our lives because this has made us stronger and inspired us to convert our adversities into empowerment. After all we are who we are today as a direct result of everything we experienced.

Foreword

Did you know that Youth unemployment is one of today's biggest global challenges?

Did you know that Youth entrepreneurship offers a solution to the above, because innovative solutions for economic growth among young people is on the increase?

First of all, I would like to identify Tray-Sean Ben Salmi as a 14-year-old teenager that I hold in high regard, not because he's my son but because I truly admire and respect him upon so many levels in the context of business and personal matters.

Tray-Sean is a remarkable teenage genius, who boosts a host of wisdom, skills, experience, products, services, unique opportunities and accolades etc. Who I have found to be passionately supportive of the work of others, devoid of triviality, and nobody's fool.

Tray-Sean Ben Salmi, prior to this book, had already made a lasting impact in both academics and his personal development. Would you agree that few teens do in our current climate of media coverage of our teens.

He participated in Child Genius and was recognised as 1 out of 20 of the smartest children in the UK for 2017, he then went on to co-author 10 Seconds to Child Genius with Philip Chan and became 1 of 34 selected to sit papers at the prestigious Eton College for Boys. For more information may I suggest that you purchase a copy of his books called I'M THAT KID – **I'M THAT KID - EMPOWERING YOU TO STEP INTO YOUR POWER FORMULA™** and 10 Seconds to Child Genius™ – From Eton Road to Eton College. At the age of 6 years old Tray-Sean launched his first short story competition in school.

Tray-Sean was 7 years old when he co-authored Kidz That Dream Big with his older sister Lashai Ben Salmi and the two of them would attend a host of prestigious investment, business development, branding and personal development events. At the time they were the only children in the room. By the age of 11 Tray-Sean was awarded an UnLtd award to run his first event called: I'm That KID – Bridging The Gap Between Fathers & Sons at Arsenal F.C. which provided a unique opportunity for fathers, their sons, Tray-Sean and his step-dad and a fundamental resetting of the moral compass.

Thanks to Tray-Sean's (and his four siblings) work, in large part, the direction of youth entrepreneurship now is beginning to point away from simply setting up business and towards helping children and young people to activate their sacred gifts, have fun, dream big and make money doing what they love while gaining key life skills, experience and unique opportunities in abundance.

As Tray-Sean's mantra says, "I'm That KID – As long as I believe in myself I can be, do and have anything I desire". This, I completely agree to be true because whatever a man thinks of most, that is exactly what he shall create.

This book is exceptional and most clearly deserves to have a very wide readership, I think it should be carefully read by every child aged 5yrs plus both locally and globally. Quite frankly, nobody else could have written this book reason being that the author himself has consistently excelled in academics and having found meaning in his life with a host of mind-blowing achievements to date (I encourage you to do some research on Tray-Sean via google).

What distinguishes this book from other books of its kind, is the fact that Tray-Sean is incredibly well connected, well informed, and a personal determination shines through every word; and yet Tray-Sean writes with the beauty of poetry. The book is so well written, it actually does deserve the worn cliché that 'I couldn't put the book down'.
Tray-Sean is an old soul in a young body, that is in affect way ahead of his time.

Tray-Sean experienced an extremely traumatic birth, which almost cost him his life. He has faced life threatening raspatory issues since birth which resulted in frequent visits to A&E and since then he has been cared for by several consultants since birth. Tray-Sean was diagnosed with Asthma at the age of 4, the precise context I am referring to the above is to highlight what a 14 year old can do, not what he or she cannot do despite being seriously ill from birth on top of having to overcome anxiety and low self-esteem.

I appreciate the sincerity, consistency, commitment, service to others, creativity, courage, passion, compassion, empathy, determination and genuineness of Tray-Sean. This book is written in a 'friendly' style, I especially recommend this book to our friends, family, colleagues and all establishments who work with children and young people. Unfortunately, our teens face a host of challenges as they transition from childhood to adulthood this endeavour should never be at the expense of the current generation of young people. I believe that the content of this book with inspire children, youth and adults alike to achieve the same or better because Tray-Sean is 'keeping it real' when it comes to highlighting what could be possible when children and youth are allowed to Dream Big as young as possible. We should all be on guard when it comes to protecting our children's natural ability to Dream Big, self-belief and experiential learning.

This book will be invaluable to anyone who wishes to learn about aspects of fully embodying their dream. I know of no other source which matches the quality and breadth of writing as in the book and the other books that Tray-Sean has authored, in a brilliant and unique way; including young onset raw creativity, personal development, self-realisation and experiential learning. And yet the book does not

9

paralyse any approach that you may currently be honouring. I recommend to you his unique chapter on Consequences of Delayed Creativity, for example. Tray's book, overall, takes the field of Youth Entrepreneurship much further forward.

In fact, the book brings up topics that I really wish I was exposed to during my own childhood, because I believe that I could have made much more progress in my life by now. In the areas of developing my core life skills, financial literacy, personal development etc as early as possible. The book introduces additional topics in a unique, incredible way so as not to make you feel uncomfortable.

One of my favourite parts of the book is About the Author, because this is where Tray-Sean shares what he has achieved to date. I believe that this will inspire others about what is possible when you choose to Dream Big, invest time in personal development and have fun learning.

I feel that through this book Tray-Sean will ultimately reach out to millions, whether they are academic, artistic and/or entrepreneurial. A word I have often heard used about Tray-Sean is 'Inspirational'. In today's society of modern-day materialism in the media, it is not uncommon for this word to be used, but in Tray's case it is richly deserved. Trays acts a focus for acknowledgement for values and attitudes which are right about this world, in generosity and warmth of spirit; of being educated, and great fun to be with. I know that family means a lot to Tray, words cannot possibly convey how proud we are of him for choosing to step into his power and embrace life despite being bullied, having low self-esteem, experiencing panic attacks due to anxiety brought on as a result of health challenges (life threatening asthma attacks) and so much more.

This book is highly original. I think it makes the weather on so many key topics, such as the natural abilities of children being just as capable as adults when it comes to entrepreneurship. Whilst it may make some people feel uncomfortable to embrace youth entrepreneurship, including 'experts' and people in the media. They need not just to hear but to listen carefully to the immense lifelong benefits of youth entrepreneurship and self-exploration. The book somehow combines being timeless, placeless, and yet firmly relevant to us all, in the here and now, and clearly ahead of its time. This inherent child/youth entrepreneurship culture does not particularly worry me, because of the sheer brilliance shared within this book.

I am truly honoured to be Tray-Sean's mum. He is the second eldest of five siblings and I must say that he inspires me and teaches me so much about life, myself and others upon a daily basis. Inside this book you'll be exposed to a host of inspiring content that could transform your life and that of children and young people around the world. Tray-Sean and his siblings are responsible for activating a host of

11

young entrepreneurs making a big stand within the world of youth Entrepreneurship.

Therefore, I truly believe that this book is a step in the right direction.

Sabrina Ben Salmi BSc, M, NLP, Hyp
Co-Founding Director of Harris Invictus, Multiple award-winning Mentor and Author, Speaker, Founder of Shift Happens, Dreaming Big Together - Mamas Secret Recipe™ and co-founder of The Conscious Entrepreneur Blueprint™

CONTENTS

INTRODUCTION.. 16
IN THE BEGINNING...17
THE JOURNEY 25
THE CHILD GENIUS APPLICATION PROCESS.........30
PARTICIPATE IN CHILD GENIUS 34
CHILD GENIIUS LIVE SHOW....................................35
CONSEQUENCES OF DELAYED CREATIVITY 38
ACTION STEPS 40
FROM CHILD GENIUS TO ETON COLLEGE.............41
EXCLUSIVE BONUS CHAPTER 46
SURPRISE BONUS: WHAT THE EXPERTS SAY... 56
ABOUT THE AUTHOR..63
ABOUT THE AUTHOR'S SIBLINGS 65

Just imagine how you'll feel as you finish reading
the last page of this book......

INTRODUCTION

I wrote this book to encourage you to go on and live your dreams; no matter where you came from: class, race, geographical location, heritage, gender etc. This book can be used as a constant reminder that it's not where you start but it's about where you choose to finish.

I desire to share my journey with you, with the aim to encourage you to fulfil your dreams and to just always go and get whatever you want in life. To always remind you that you can do, be and have anything that you desire in life as long as you believe in yourself.

IN THE BEGINNING

I grew up on Eton Road, Ilford IG1, we moved there on 24/9/2007 and moved out 25/2/2017. I lived there with my mum, step-dad and 5 siblings (my nan also lived with us for a couple of years until she had to become a carer for my grate nan). We had a spacious open plan 3-bedroom house with a massive garden. The interior was painted in magnolia with chocolate brown skirting boards and banister and we had chocolate brown carpet throughout our home. Once you entered our home you'd see our staircase that led upstairs to a huge bathroom which housed our toilet, shower and bath. Then my two sisters shared a room, my parents room was next and then the boys room which I shared with my younger brother.

I come from a large family, therefore you can imagen that we experienced a host of ups and downs just like any other family. I really love being a part of a big family because there is always something to do and someone to do it with. We are all very different in our own unique way. Nan was the one who would always splash out on expensive designer items and would always get us out of trouble when we did something wrong. One of the things that my nan would often say is "Leave them, they didn't do nothing wrong – they're just kids. Are you okay my Tu-tu-luts/darling/push/du-duts?".

If I am honest nan would say this all the time even when we did something wrong and I would just smile because mum wouldn't buy it, even if she would have to listen to nan out of respect. My step-dad was strict and enjoyed cooking. Mum spent a lot of time on personal development and raising us, she was easy going and it took her many years to speak her truth. Now that bring me on to Lashai, she's the one to watch because she was the one really in charge. We all listened to Lashai and she always knew how to get what she wanted no matter what. I'm the second sibling in line and I was just quiet and learned through observation. Yasmine is a loving and caring character and would always teach us to love more. Paolo is fearless and would always push the boundaries even when we told him not to and then there is little Amire. As the saying goes, size doesn't matter, I am beginning to believe that that saying was coined because of my little bro because he is totally unaware of limits, boundaries and fears. Therefore, I am sure that you could imagine what our day to day life was life ha, ha, ha, ha…

Downstairs was our open planned lounge and dining room that led to our galley kitchen. Our dining room backed onto our garden. In our garden we were able to fit so many things in it we had a trampoline, electric cars, football table, swing set, a see-saw and so much more. It was probably where we spent most of our time when it wasn't raining. We played there, we had parties there, we would have family dinners/BBQs during summer. In our house there was always that smell of either strawberries or the smell of cinnamon. Whilst

17

growing up we didn't get to socialise much locally because the neighbours kept themselves to themselves. I can recall having a couple of sleepover at my best friend's (Alfie) home. Where we lived our neighbours were very unfriendly, and when we played football in our garden if we kicked the ball over (which happened a lot) they would either chuck our ball in their shed or they would pop our ball. Eventually we stopped playing football in our garden to prevent that from happening.

My Nan (Mary Paul) always wanted us to
Look our best and was always making sure that we had designer clothing and suits. I really appreciate all that my mum and grandma have done and continue to do for us.

I attended a local school in Redbridge. Unfortunately, I didn't have the best of experiences in primary school because I was often bullied. For example, in one of our lessons pencil lead was put in to my ear and it hurt a lot, things like this would happen upon a daily basis – if I tried to defend myself I would get into trouble. So, I decided to ignore them and just focus on completing my school work so I could go into and remain in top set, eventually I was put onto the gifted and talented list. Can you remember a time when you had to pick your battles so you could move towards your desired outcomes?

I would often cry in school because I would frequently be targeted just because I was smart. I realised that I had to make friends with some of the popular kids in order to survive and I could help them with their maths. I also became good at football, which really helped to make me popular. Finally, I grew to know a lot of people who would always look out for me and who would protect both myself and my siblings if anything was to happen. I was chosen to join our school football team and it was such a remarkable feeling to be on our school team. I have always loved to play football come wind, rain, snow or sleet – nothing could get in the way of me playing football. It was so much fun because we would often win. Outside of school I took football seriously by training daily to make sure that I stay fit and strong to ensure that I can always perform at my best.

I am a big believer of the saying that my eldest sister taught me 'practice makes improvement'

Would you agree that it is always a good idea to practice whatever you desire to master?

I had a traumatic birth and ever since then I have had respiratory problems. I was always in and out of the hospital so much so that I was known by the ambulance operators, ambulance paramedics and hospital staff. As a result, I would miss a lot of school. The good thing is I always stayed in top set because studying has always been something that I enjoy.

What do you enjoy doing?

What do you spend most of your time practicing?

Just know, that whatever you spend time on and focus on the most you will eventually master it and then go on to develop your own unique artistry.

The question is what will you become a master of as a result of what you have been doing daily?

Spending quality time together has always been one of our core family values. This meant a host of trips to Tunisia, Portugal and Chessington World of Adventures. LEGOLAND, Under 17 Car Driving, London Eye and London Dungeons. The River Themes Clipper boat, hosting workshops, speaking on stage, Greenwich Park, Science Museum, Barbican, Ice Skating, featuring in TV shows, newspapers, radio, writing books and Swimming.

Unique opportunities and gifts, Horse Riding, Natural History Museum, British Museum and the British Library to name a few. I looked forward to every weekend because we always had so much fun spending time together as a family.

One of my fondest memories is when my mum took us away to Portugal for my sisters birthday. We had so much fun in Lisbon with friends (Barbosa Family: Barbra, husband, Guilherme and Margarida), we stayed in their amazing four-story home. We had an amazing experience there as it was a private gated complex with a swimming pool, football court, basketball court, park, gym, football table etc.

we would wake up at the crack of dawn and played until the last one was standing. We had so many friends and even if some of us couldn't speak the same language, that didn't stop us from having fun.

Can you remember a time when you had so much fun and didn't want the night to end?

My childhood has been and still is pretty amazing and at times I just have to express gratitude and pinch myself.

Whilst doing all of these amazing things both myself and my older sister (Lashai), were doing work experience with **Miles Fryer** and **Sammy Blindell** in their branding company called '**How to Build Your Brand**'. We worked with them for two years. We were also fortunate to be surrounded by a host of coaches, mentors and trainings.

The interesting thing is, I selected Business Enterprise as a GCSE option and on the first day we had to do an assessment and my teacher was blown away by my extensive knowledge within branding, business, social media, media and marketing. I was allocated an expected grade of A* and he asked where I acquired my extensive knowledge and I proudly replied that I've been doing work experience with our family friends called **Miles Fryer** and **Sammy Blindell** in their branding company called '**How to Build Your Brand**'.

The teacher contacted my mum to commend me and I am pleased to say that she was touched by my teachers excitement towards me. I also managed to join a football team call Redbridge FC thanks to Chris (Alfie's dad). Alfie was small and the other players would make fun of him pre-match – Alfie and I would just laugh because he was on fire once he touched the ball because his dad trained him as soon as he could walk. We were both stickers and we would enjoy being silent and allowing our actions to speak loudly because we had great chemistry within our team we were at the top of our league, and we lost very few matches.

I can remember a time when I was the star of the match. One of my favourite memories was when my Redbridge FC coach came to our home to collect me for training, due to an Arsenal F.C. scout coming to watch me. There were a few times that he had attended, but I wasn't there because I was unwell and had difficulties breathing so couldn't attend training.

My coached informed my mum and I that the scout liked me and the words he used was 'Tay-Sean is a born athlete; anyone can be taught technical skills - but athletes are born'. When I was well enough to attend training and match days the Arsenal F.C scout returned and was watching me play, unfortunately it wasn't one of my best games because I had lost my favourite football boots in transit to the match, I had to play in my spare boots that were meant for indoors. These boots didn't have much grip, so I kept slipping and sliding all over the place!

Can you remember a time when you wished that you had a better plan B?

How do you tend to react or respond when things don't go according to plan. I must say that I felt devastated when I wasn't scouted, but I chose to focus on building my dreams no matter what.

THE JOURNEY

I can still remember the day that I returned from school and my mum sat me down to inform me that she had submitted an application for me to participate in Child Genius.

At the time we hadn't watched the show so I didn't really know what to expect. As a family we would often participate in a variety of TV, newspapers, magazines, radio and other media therefore I was open to the experience.

I really enjoyed the entire process from day one until the live show, because it was so much fun. The Child Genius team were so friendly and fun to talk to, we enjoyed all the filming, all the interviews, I absolutely loved the tests and the open day. Prior to the live show competition days, me and my entire family were booked into an all expenses paid hotel. We took a taxi to the hotel, our breakfast lunch and dinner was also paid for and in the hotel the was a gym, swimming pool, sauna and steam room. My family and I had such a fantastic time. We were treated like celebrities throughout the process.

THE CHILD GENIUS APPLICATION PROCESS

When completing the form, be sure to give detailed answers. If they are interested in finding out more about you, they will then contact you to verify the parent or the legal guardian, and that you have consented to the submission of the application. They would then like to hear a little bit more about you and your family's motivation for entering the competition. Should the Child Genius team wish to proceed further still with the application they would ask for a photo of you and of the family and they would organise a time to conduct a video interview with your entire family, via Skype or FaceTime. (This can be done by telephone if video calling is not possible).

Child Genius 2017 featured a competition devised in association with high IQ society British Mensa and other leading children's educational experts. Around 20 brilliant 8-12-year olds took part in rounds. The Child Genius team will spend time filming with you and your family in the lead-up to the start of the competition, between rounds and in preparation for the grand finale.

Each of the six episodes will follow a number of children taking part in the competition. (Unfortunately, the Child Genius team cannot guarantee that everyone will be included or the extent to which they will be included in the finished series). They will explore with parents the joys and challenges of raising a gifted child. It is important that the Child Genius team will be able to tell the individual story of each family featured – how attitudes to parenting and schooling may differ from one parent to another.

The Child Genius team are also really keen to appeal to children who have the ability, but until now have never had the chance to shine – children of all backgrounds with different interests, academic and non-academic, are welcome to apply.

Child Genius offers parents the chance to bring their children together with like-minded peers.

The 2017 Child Genius competition took place at London's Royal Institution, near Green Park.

MORE ABOUT THE CHILD GENIUS SELECTION PROCESS

The application process involves FIVE stages:

An application form. They will review all applications and may follow up those applications with a Skype/FaceTime or phone chat with the family one early evening after school.

Those selected to go forward will be invited to a Child Genius Open Day in London. The children (with accompanying families) will register, meet producers and circulate round various rooms where they can show off their abilities or even discover some new hidden potential. Activities will include (but are not limited to): Fingers-on-Buzzers quizzing; the Mensa Challenge; Strategy Games and Logic Puzzles. Child Genius producers, educational psychologists and a representative from Mensa will be on hand to answer your questions. After the lunchtime period, children will sit a Raven's Matrices paper (a long-established non-verbal multiple-choice test of general intelligence). Your child's results will be posted to you for your personal information once the series has been filmed and broadcast. General filming will take place at this Open Day.

The Child Genius team will arrange home visits for those families proceeding to the next stage of the application process. This will be a chance for the Child Genius team to get a sense of life at home and will be a first small taste of the cameras for the family. This is a great chance for children to show the Child Genius team some of their hobbies and interests – this was something that I really enjoyed taking part in.

A shortlist of families will then be selected to attend a series of meetings at Wall to Wall's offices. This is where I sat a one-on-one IQ test with an educational psychologist and there was a private consultation for my whole family with a clinical psychologist. My families also had an in-depth private chat with the series' senior editorial team, to answer any questions about, and discuss generally, future participation in the competition and the

31

series. They had to speak to both of my parents, they also offered to organise a separate meeting for any parent who couldn't attend on this day for any reason, so that he or she can feel fully informed first-hand. From here the Child Genius team feel that all parties will have the tools to make an informed decision as to whether taking part in the competition and the series is right for you and your family.

Using the information gathered during the application process, up to 20 children and their families will be selected and invited to take part in the televised competition. Please note that wide and varied criteria will be used to make the final decision as to those children selected to take part in the competition including (without limitation) academic tests; a range of interests; hobbies; attitudes to learning and different educational beliefs. The producer and broadcaster's decision is final.

My family and I were beyond excited when we were informed that I had made the preshow shortlist, then when we were informed that I had been selected to be one of the 20 children to make it onto the live show. Now, that was the difference that made the difference and we were all excited, we played music danced around and played and laughed the entire night. I felted overwhelmed with joy because it was Philip Chan who told me to apply and he attended the live show to support me and some of his other friends. beyond excited when

PARTICIPATE IN CHILD GENIUS

Throughout my life I have been taught to say yes to aligned opportunities and to also create opportunities. As a child I encourage you to take all opportunities that can add to your CV/personal profile. In life I believe that you should seek all opportunities that grow you and also allow you to explore your natural talents because you never know what doors can be presented to you.

The unique aspect of participating in Child Genius is the fact that you are able to gain national credibility for your academic performance which can go on to be presented to private schools, grammar schools, colleges and universities. This is what led me to be invited to sit papers at the prestigious Eton College.

I believe that you should apply to participate in Child Genius because it'll be the difference that makes the difference to your life in so many ways. After all you have nothing to lose and absolutely everything to gain.

Just imagine how different your life could be if you gave yourself permission to expand your comfort zone, have fun learning, and follow your dreams while you surrender to the natural and organic unfoldment of life.

#whytrytofitinwhenyouwereborntostandout

CHILD GENIUS LIVE SHOW

Channel 4's Child Genius is hosted by Pointless star Richard Osman, it was such a pleasure to meet him and his team. The Child Genius show consists of 20 of the brightest 8 -12 year old kids in Britain that go on to battle it out, in a series of mind-challenging tests, devised in association with high-IQ society Mensa and some of the world's leading educational bodies, in the hope of being crowned Child Genius. The 2017 episodes were recorded at London's Royal Institution, near Green Park tube.

It was the morning of the live show, the first day of the competition. All of the interviews, all of the tests, all of the preparation has led to this very day. I woke up feeling unusually tense and fearful, I had countless thoughts rushing through my mind.

Me, mum, step-dad, nan and four siblings had our showers, got dressed and then ate breakfast together. Our transportation arrived just after breakfast to transport us to London's Royal Institution, near Green Park tube. Despite previously doing this trip before, this time round it was different. The journey seems to take longer, I felt different and this time there was a huge crowd queuing up to get inside, there were cameras everywhere and the cameras welcomed us as we pulled up to the London's Royal Institution building.

I had made it to the live show, and everything felt different, it used to be fun and exciting however that feeling of fun had entirely dissipated. I was living the dream, but yet I felt awful inside, can you remember a time when you felt mixed emotions when you should feel on top of the world? When we entered the waiting area you could see the stress on everyone's faces, oh wow to say that the pressure was on is an understatement.

I was sweating, I felt dizzy, my chest felt tight and I felt as if I was about to faint. Giselle Malawer came to support me to deal with the stress by giving me an Alexander Technique to help me to reduce the stress in my body.

We played games to help me to relax (one of the games we played was Race to Infinity designed by Grace Olugbodi). Prior to going live for the first element of the competition I had to go for a walk with my mum and psychologist as he wanted me to pull out of the competition because I was showing signs of stress. I pleaded with him and my mum to allow me to at least try. They agreed to allow me to continue providing that I was be honest with them about how I really felt prior to and following each competition round.

It was only day one of the contest and I was out that's right, I was out. As soon as I was eliminated, I felt amazing, it was as if a weight had been lifted from my shoulders. I came to realize that I had previously felt stressed due to the meaning that I had chosen to subscribe to the experience. This made me feel extremely proud of myself for making it on to the live because each and every child who made it this far had to pass a series of Mensa IQ testings. Therefore all 20 of us were recognized as the top 20 of the smartest children in the UK. To say that it was a proud moment in my life is an understatement.

As a result of participating in Child Genius I went on to be 1 out of 34 boys in the entire UK to be invited to sit entry papers at the prestigious Eton College for Boys in Windsor. This was totally mind blowing upon so many levels. To find out more purchase a copy of my book called 10 Seconds to Child Genius - From Eton Road to Eton College

Please see below a brief of each contest day (You can watch all of the Child Genius episodes via: https://www.channel4.com/programmes/child-genius/on-demand/65319-001)

Series 2017 Episode 1
The new contest begins with the demanding Spelling round and the complex Linguistic Memory round - testing the kids with the scientific names of 60 fruit and vegetables. You can watch this episode online and it lasts 47 mins.

Series 2017 Episode 2
It's day two of the week-long competition as the kids face a testing Maths round and also a complex Memory challenge featuring a London bus map.

You can watch this episode online and it lasts 47 mins.

Series 2017 Episode 3
The remaining 13 kids face two challenging History rounds, including Ancient Greece to the modern day, and the British royal family. You can watch this episode online and it lasts 47 mins.

Series 2017 Episode 4
It's the quarter-final in this week-long competition to find Britain's brightest child and quizmaster Richard Osman tests the remaining 11 kids on Science and Memory. You can watch this episode online and it lasts 47 mins.

Series 2017 Episode 5
It's the semi-final in this week-long competition and the eight remaining competitors face two of the toughest rounds yet with Advanced Language and a sudden-death Spelling test. You can watch this episode online and it lasts 47 mins.

Series 2017 Episode 6
The five finalists face two demanding rounds, including a quick-fire buzzer session, as they bid to be crowned Child Genius of 2017. You can watch this episode online and it lasts 47 mins

CONSEQUENCES OF DELAYED CREATIVITY

I believe that there are significant consequences of delayed creativity. As it'll have a huge negative impact on your financial education, personal development, network, experiential learning, unique opportunities, pocket money and it'll deprive you of priceless experiences that you could have had.

Creativity promotes personal expression, neuroscience and cognitive science research are constantly providing information that links creativity with intelligence; academic, social, emotional intelligence; and the development of skill sets and the highest information processing that will become increasingly valuable for children and youth.

In my view allowing children to discover their unique essence of creativity as young as possible is the difference that makes the difference.

Did you know that creative expression impacts our conceptual thinking and transfer of knowledge, judgment, recognition of relationships for symbolic conceptualisation, self-evaluation of emotions, including recognising and analysing response choices and the ability to recognize and activate memories.

Take a moment to reflect on the impact that the lack of or the abundance of creativity has had on your life?

ACTION STEPS

Take a moment to reflect on all of the content that you have been exposed to in this book and then choose three *Action Steps*

1.
2.
3.

Give each *Action Steps* a deadline date

1.
2.
3.

How will you know when you have successfully achieved each of your *Action Steps*?

1.
2.
3.

FROM CHILD GENIUS TO ETON COLLEGE

Wow! Wow! Wow!

Where on Earth do I begin?.... one thing that I must say is that it does not matter where you start, what matters most is where you choose to go.

The application process was extraordinarily phenomenal. Eton College surpassed all my expectations of a full boarding school and then some. Firstly, I was rendered speechless when I saw that the school spans over such a large area not like anything I've seen before. I can only describe it as a village as opposed to a boarding school. Different academic subject. departments are located on various roads.

How cool is that?....

Visiting the site has totally blown my mind. The staff support from start to finish were so warm, professional and supportive upon so many levels.

Somebody pinch me because I have been invited to sit papers at the prestigious Eton College, Windsor and I'm 1 of 34 boys in the entire UK (that's roughly a ratio of 1 in 100,000 boys)

Obviously just like any relationship, there are elements of privacy and confidentiality that cannot be violated, in order to uphold respect for Eton college. So, unfortunately I'll not be able to tell you about the testing procedure. All I can say is that I highly recommend that you and everyone you know do some research on what it takes for a boy to apply to Eton College, because it'll totally transform your perspective on education as it did for me, my mum, and brothers when we attended.

I can still remember our journey to Eton College, the way they greeted us, the manner in which the boys conducted themselves, the positive thoughts that were running through my mind and that warm fuzzy feeling in my tommy really made me feel like it was my home. I can remember what we had for lunch, the Q & A session, the way they treated us, the way in which they poetically spoke about education and the life time impact that they have on all the boys who become Etonians. I convey absolute gratitude for such a truly remarkable experience and memories, that I will cherish for a lifetime.

Eton College staff were amazing really kind towards all of us. They were open to answering all of our questions.

When I found out that I hadn't passed the test, I immediately realised where I had messed up. I was nervous and rushing and did not read all of the information properly. This was my first experience

41

with academics at such a prestigious level. I didn't know how to prepare myself. As the saying goes, if you fail to plan - you're planning to fail. I felt really down because I had seen how serious they were about sports and academic studies, I really wanted to get in. what was interesting is the fact that I was 13 and only recently heard about the school, however some boys are put onto the waiting list at birth and their cut off point for applications is year 5 – so how lucky was I to have had the opportunity… finding this information out made me feel extremely proud of myself for being invited and giving it my best shot, especially due to the fact that I was raised in Eton Road and made it all the way to Eton College despite my challenges, background, class and financial background etc. so you see, never give up, because you have no idea where your efforts can lead to in the end.

My mum explained to me that everything happens for a reason, maybe it wasn't the right time for me (as I was facing serious health challenges that could have cost my life as it's a boarding school) and that I should always remember that as one door closes another shall open. It truly was life changing experience for me and two younger brothers. I really appreciate the fact that I was able to have such an experience with my brothers and mum right by my side to support me through the process. My little brothers were able to see what is possible for them when they choose to work smart. I see all of my opportunities as blessings and a glimpse of what is available when we choose to expand.

Did you know that Eton was founded in 1440 by King Henry VI as "Kynge's College of Our Ladye of Eton besyde Windesore" to provide free education to 70 poor boys who would then go on to King's College, Cambridge, which he founded 1441.

Eton promotes the best habits of independent thought and learning in the pursuit of excellence; provides a broadly-based education designed to enable all boys to discover their strengths, and to make the most of their talents within Eton and beyond. Eton engenders respect for individuality, difference, the importance of teamwork and the contribution that each boy makes to the life of the school and the community; supporting pastoral care that nurtures physical health, emotional maturity and spiritual richness and fostering self-confidence, enthusiasm, perseverance, tolerance, integrity and so much more.

Did you know that Prince Harry, Prince William aand Sir John Edward Nourse Heygate, 4th Baronet Heygate (19 April 1903 – 18 March 1976) was a Northern Irish journalist and novelist attended Eton College?

EXCLUSIVE BONUS CHAPTER

There is a saying that your network equals, YOUR NET WORTH. I am certainly fortunate to be surrounded by a host of extraordinarily, phenomenal and incredible people. Therefore, I asked three of our family friends these four questions:

1.   If you were to give advice to your younger self what would it be?

2.   What are you really proud of?

3.   What would you want to change?

4.   What challenges occurred at my age (14) and what did you do to overcome them?

DR. BREMLEY W.B. LYNGDOH
(family friend)

Founder and Chief Executive of Worldview Impact Foundation

Dr. Bremley W.B. Lyngdoh is the Founder and CEO of Worldview Impact Foundation. He is a Climate Change and Sustainable Development professional with over 20 years' experience working with Governments, IGOs, NGOs and the Private Sector developing a range of innovative projects in Asia, Africa and South America aimed at producing ecologically sound and economically viable activities that contribute directly to reducing rural poverty, and generating productive sustainable livelihoods for vulnerable local communities. Bremley has all the relevant experience in project sourcing and development. His strength lies in building strategic partnerships with various governmental agencies, NGOs and multilateral development agencies. Through his previous assignments working with the United Nations and the World Bank in Asia, Africa and Latin America, he has gained expertise in the effective monitoring and evaluation of field-based programmes. Bremley developed projects on climate change adaptation, integrated agroforestry, sustainable tourism and renewable energy.

- Charity fund raising event running the Paris marathon for the Children's Trust https://www.thechildrenstrust.org.uk/
- You can support our projects by donating on http://worldviewimpact.org/causes/

46

- You can offset your carbon footprint by buying a rubber trees on http://worldviewimpact.com/login.php

1) If you were to give advice to your younger self what would it be?

Keep your dreams alive no matter what happens along the way and give your best each day. We need to have a powerful revolution in our hearts to create a beautiful evolution in our minds.

2) What are you really proud of?

I am very proud that Indian Prime Minister Atal Bihari Vajpayee appointed me as the Youth Representative for India during the historic United Nations Millennium Summit where I addressed world leaders during Millennium Assembly on 28th September 2000 at the UN HQ in New York.

3) What would you want to change?

If I could go back in time I would spend more time with my father in India who died from a heart attack in 2012 during his early morning run in the forest. If I had been running with him that morning I would have been able to save him and he would be still alive today.

4) What challenges occurred at my age (14) and what did you do to overcome them?

I was having challenges with balancing high school work while I was studying at St. Edmund's School in Shillong and working in my family farm to earn some pocket money. I lost my focus in time management so I joined the school musical and rebuilt my confidence by learning to perform in front of a big public audience.

JUERGEN PALLIEN
(my stock & trading mentor)

Juergen Pallien is a Master of Automation! His ability to automate success in Business and Investing creates financial liberation to pursue the most exciting and important things in life! Juergen has used automation as the key strategy for success in his career as a serial entrepreneur, international speaker, property mogul, stock market investor and now, as a philanthropist.

Described as a Financial Liberation Genius with a Comedian's sense of humour, Juergen is on a mission to help 1 Million people achieve their own financial liberation! Educated by some of Europe's most renowned Universities in Management, Information Technology, Sales, Influence and Leadership, Juergen is fanatical about personal and professional growth and coaching. He believes that which is not growing, is dying!

Juergen is BEST known for using automation to create efficiencies in Sales, Business Growth and customer focused problem solving that led him to build and sell several companies and retire by the age of 35.

Fascinated by the stock market since he first traded in 1998, Juergen studied the investment strategies of Warren Buffett, Robert Kiyosaki and George Soros. Building on their knowledge, he has now invented several proven strategies to easily and predictably earn money without the need to sit in front of a computer all day. Juergen is committed to sharing his stock market success formulas to help

One Million people put their financial success on auto-pilot and live their passion!

When he is not helping others, Juergen likes to do sports, play chess, listen to music and read lots of books.

For your questions or to learn how you can become 1 of Juergen's million beneficiaries, contact him directly at:

- YouTube: www.youtube.com/channel/UCiFeVHbloS PO0wqWZTx8gIg/videos
- Website: www.24hprofits.com
- www.facebook.com/juergen.pallien.1
- www.twitter.com/j_pallien
- www.linkedin.com/in/jpallien

1) If you were to give advice to your younger self what would it be?

Learn to invest properly and the power of compounding. Also, to only buy luxury goods and fun stuff from the earnings of your investments rather than your net worth.

2) What are you really proud of?

The results of my students who never had any experience with the stock market but tripled their investment within in the first 10 months or were able to quit their job after just 8 months.

3) What would you want to change?

Financially liberate 1 million people in the world to enable them to live their passion and make it a better place for everyone.

4) What challenges occurred at my age (14) and what did you do to overcome them?

I was living in a very small village that limited my possibilities. I'd love to help young people on their entrepreneurial journey and provide them with the knowledge and infrastructure to make their bright ideas become a reality no matter what background they have. Everyone deserves an equal chance in life.

REGAN HILLYER
(my personal development & business mentor)

Regan Hillyer is a Serial Entrepreneur, Philanthropist, Mindset Coach and Global Speaker. She is the founder of Regan Hillyer International, a company dedicated to providing personal development and business training to men and women who have a big message they want to share with the world.

Regan specialises in helping experts uncover their true message and launch powerful personal brands, helping them make a big impact and build a legacy. Regan has trained thousands of people, helping them build multiple six and seven figure businesses location free, using powerful mindset changing tools and cutting edge business development strategies.

Regan is a certified Master of NLP, Master of Hypnosis, Time Dynamics Specialist and a Success Strategist, amongst completing many other certifications and trainings. Regan has invested in excess of half a million dollars on her own personal development and business journey and takes pride in continuously learning and growing from key industry leaders.

- www.reganhillyer.com/shop

1) If you were to give advice to your younger self what would it be?

Trust yourself. Really trust yourself. All of the answers are within you and you are able to access all of these answers at any age!

2) What are you really proud of?

I'm really proud of the relationships I have in my life. My fiancé, my family relationships, my friends, my clients, my community. I am always surrounded by high vibrational people online and offline and it's taken work, but my relationships mean everything to me.

3) What would you want to change?

I'm always looking to change the number of people that I'm impacting every year.

There are so many people in the world who I want to help, and it fills me up when I am able to impact and serve at a greater level!

4) What challenges occurred at my age (14) and what did you do to overcome them?

At 14 I had no idea what I wanted to do with my life. I felt overwhelmed and confused when people asked me.

Bonus Question for my mentor:

5) What did you want to be when you grow up?

I would make up answers to try and please adults, when really, I had no idea. I went down a path of really figuring out what my purpose was in this world by diving deeper into books and personal development, and I chose to be okay with not knowing all of the answers even when people wanted me to have answers!

SURPRISE BONUS: WHAT THE EXPERTS SAY

Feng Shui to help support children, especially those having a hard time at school by Master Sarah McAllister - a Feng Shui consultant and horoscope specialist with over 14 years' experience.

A bullied kid will be suffering from fear and lack of confidence, so you really need to make sure their home environment is supportive.

Bedroom Tips to Create a Supportive Space

If possible give children separate beds, not bunk beds as they tend to feel oppressed by either the ceiling or the top bunk. Wooden bed frames are preferable to metal ones and make sure the beds have good solid headboards. Place beds so there is a nice solid wall behind the headboard - this helps the child feel more secure. Their back is literally covered.

Study Tips

Place desks so that the chair has its back to a solid wall and child is overlooking the room or preferably looking out a window to the side too. Don't place desk against the bedroom wall to save on space, otherwise the kid is facing a brick wall, both actually and metaphorically speaking! Allow kids to study at kitchen table, as sometimes they just need to have people nearby in order to concentrate.

Respect their gut instincts

Little people have very good instincts and will know what colour they want in their room or where they want to sit to study, respect this always.

Put their artwork and pictures of friends on the bedroom wall

It sounds obvious, but some parents overlook this and leave a child's room bare and austere. Kids (and adults) **LOVE** to see images of their friends and also symbols of their success around them. Ideally place these pictures above eye level, as looking upwards activates vision and aspiration, whereas looking downwards concentrates us in the past.

Keep Electronics at a minimum in their bedroom

Electrical alarm clocks, cordless phones, mobile phones, computers - all must be either switched off or kept out of the bedroom so that the energy can settle during the night time and not interfere with the delicate bioelectrical field of your child which is still developing.

Use Natural Paints & Organic Materials if possible

Indoor air can be more polluted than outdoor air, so a good air filter is recommended, and use of natural paints. Chemical paints and artificial fabrics can create allergies in your child. The last thing they need is a skin condition or unsightly reactions due to allergies when they are already feeling vulnerable at school.

Use Chinese Horoscope Wisdom to help your child

Ask us to 'open the horoscope' of your child - we can decipher whether there is the presence of unhelpful authority (bullying) in the chart and advise colours to wear (as underwear if they have to wear a uniform), little pictures or totem animals to carry with them to support their chi, what foods are helpful to them and which directions within the house are best to occupy. *We had one mum from Croydon concerned with the amount of tickings off her son was getting at school, and my students and I went around to do a case study, moved his bed to a more empowering position and lo and almost overnight there was no more trouble. I also helped a kiddie in Holland Park to sleep through the night (previously waking up at 4am and bouncing into the parents room!) just by moving her bed to a more supportive area of the room and aligning it to 'quiet' energy as opposed to 'active' energy.*

Another young boy with Attention Deficit Disorder was immediately helped by moving the position of his bed and performing a space clearing - the father was initially sceptical but developed a respect for what I had done based on the results he had witnessed.

This type of refined, intricate and powerful classical Feng Shui is not a self-help subject - the above pointers are useful basics, but don't substitute a professional Feng Shui consultation and horoscope analysis. For further information please visit www.myfengshuifriend.com

email info@fengshuiagency.com

I URGE YOU TO DREAM BIG

Having **dream**s can make you feel happy. The more important that your **dream**s are to you, the more you will want to hold on to it!!
I want you to take a moment to think about what you would do if you weren't afraid to have **FUN**, **DREAM BIG** and make **money** doing what you **LOVE**? That's right... Just go ahead and allow yourself to feel your deepest and wildest **dream**s deep within your heart. After all we all have **dream**s... right? Yes or No? Fear simply holds you back. Remember you are a *creator*, when you choose to move beyond your fears you can begin to feel free.
If you don't change you can become extinct, let's face it... change is always happening. Each and every day visualise your **dream**s as often as possible... imagine yourself enjoying your **dream**s because it can lead you to it. Movement in a new direction can help you achieve your **dream**s... so don't worry too much about being different to your peers. Difference is also good, so follow your own **dream**s and remain true to yourself. The quicker you let go of peer pressure and your old negative values and beliefs, the sooner you can find new positive values and beliefs that will serve you well. When your values and beliefs change so will your life. It will serve you best to pursue your **dream**s instead of simply living your life in default mode following your peers etc. We both know that holding onto old negative values and beliefs will not lead you to new positive results. When you realise

that you can achieve your **dream**s, your life will begin to transform if you choose to. Acknowledging small change early can help you to adept to **big**ger changes that are to come, simply allow your **dream**s to flow and then you can begin your dance with the universe.

Sabrina Ben Salmi BSc

WORDS FROM THE HEART OF A NAN

Parents: You have to help our children and youth, because they are tomorrow's leaders. If your child has a **dream,** you must help them to nurture that seed for it to grow. Without TLC that seed cannot grow and your Childs' **dream** will surely die. It is not about pushing or pressuring your child. Ask your child how you can be of assistance and best support them to grow their **dream**? If you notice that your child is reaching out for support with a desire to be creative. Encourage them in each and every way, but always remember that it is your child's **dream** not yours. Also, too much pressure could disrupt their creative process. Take one step at a time and enjoy the experience with them. Simply embrace this priceless experience together and give them a little independence as this will help them to learn valuable life lessons along the way.

Children and Youth: If you have a **dream** don't let anyone take your **dream** away from you because that **dream** is yours and it was created by you and no one but you has the ability to breathe life into your **dream**. Always believe in yourself and your **dream**s 100%. There is no such thing as too young; even if you are 5 years old give it your all. In the end at least you will know that you have at least tried your best.

Mary Paul

((((CONGRATULATIONS))))

Trust yourself, as you k**now so** more than you think you do. Simply inhale inspiration and exhale action. **G**o ahead and do what you k**now** you ought to do. The answer you have always been waiting for is yes you can, do, be and have whatever your heart desires.

It is an absolute honour to welcome you to our family. What are you going to do to celebrate your achievements?

ABOUT THE AUTHOR

AS SEEN OF TV, RADIO & NEWSPAPERS

Tray-Sean Ben Salmi aka I'm That KID is not your average 14yr old. Tray-Sean Ben Salmi is a 14yr old Amazon No.1 Award Winning Author, Public Speaker Award Winning, Presented award for TruLittle Heros Award 2018, Guest Speaker at The Beat You Expo, Multi-award winning child advocate, Made For Mums Judge 2018, former member of Team Trouble (participated in campaigns for Sainsburys, Legoland, Warner Bros, Sony and Made For Mums to name a few) founded by Shadia Daho, Amazing Arabella & JD The Super Car Kid, Child Genius 2017 1 of 20 smartest children in the UK, 1 of 34 boys invited to sit at the prestigious Eton College for Boys.

Official Judge for Made For Mums Toy Awards 2018 via Team Trouble, An award winning author of Kidz That Dream Big, Former Radio Show host, Regan Hillyer International Be Your Brand Fellow, Author of 10 Seconds To Child Genius, Winner of TruLittle Heros Award - Academic 2017, Public speaker, a business/personal developments mentor & coach and founder of I'm That KID Blueprint covers:

- I'm That KID - Bridging the Gap Between Fathers & Sons
- I'm That KID – Creating A Vision Board for My Future

- I'm That KID – Taking to The Stage
- I'm That KID - Inspiring My Community to Pay It Forward
- I'm That KID - There's A Book Inside ME
- I'm That KID - Families That Play Together, Stay Together
- I'm That KID - Empowering You to Step into Your POWER
- I'm That KID - BEING the Change That I Desires to See in The World

And co-founder of 10 Seconds to Child Genius who is here to help child to plant the seed to create a brighter Future. Tray-Sean's signature program: I'M That KID Blueprint™

BEN SALMI FAMILY MANTRA
BEN SALMI TEAMWORK MAKES THE DREAMWORK.
We believe that there is no such thing as failure only feedback.
We also believe that the journey of one thousand miles begins with a single step in the right direction
FAMILY ANTHEM
If you want to be somebody,
If you want to go somewhere,
You better wake up and PAY ATTENTION
I'm ready to be somebody,
I'm ready to go somewhere,
I'm ready to wake up and PAY ATTENTION!
The question is *ARE* *YOU?*

ABOUT TRAY-SEAN'S SIBLINGS

AS SEEN OF TV, RADIO & NEWSPAPERS

Lashai Ben Salmi aka DREAMPRENEUR is not your average 18yr old. She is a multi-award winning Youth Advocate, Presented award for TruLittle Heros Award 2018, Content Creator for The Korean Cultural Centre, Winner of TruLittle Heros Award - Entrepreneur 2017, Speaker at Virgin Money Lounge Historical Black History Month first ever event, Guest Speaker at The Beat You Expo, Guest Speaker at Mercedes Benz World 10th April 2018, High Profile Club, YouTuber with 25K plus subscribers and over 4M plus views (Korean Channel), An award winning author of Kidz That Dream Big, Andy Harrington ACE Coach, Former International Radio Show host, Winner of Regan Hillyer International Scholarship, a speaker, a business/personal developments mentor & coach, founder of Blossom Tree Photography & Videography (Produced content for Shadia Daho for Amazing Arabella, JD The Super Kid & Team Trouble in association with Legoland Resort, Harry Potter, Little Mix and Disney Pixar, Sony, Warner Brothers & Universal etc.) co-founder of A Precipice of A Dream and founder of Put The RED Card Up To bullying & My Journey - Giving Youth Several Reasons to Smile who is here to help children and youth to plant the seed for an abundance of unique opportunities via a variety of products and services to assist you to create a brighter future

Lashai has been mentored by some of the leading name within the personal development world Regan Hillyer, Andy Harrington, Cheryl Chapman, Harry Singha, Ralph Plumb, Sammy Blindell to name a few. Lashai has shared the stage with the likes of the late Dr. Miles Monrune, Dr. John Demartini, Andy Harrington, Robert G Allen and Ralph Plumb to name a few.

If you are looking for an inspiring, wise, talented, refreshing and powerful speaker then 18yr old Lashai Ben Salmi is guaranteed to make a big impact at your event. Lashai has been a part of the personal development world since the age of 11yrs. Lashai has a burning desire to transform lives with her stage presence, knowledge and wisdom! Lashai's signature topics include: Congruency, Alignment, Self-Belief, YouTube, Social Media, Connection, Inspiration and Motivation.
Lashai's signature program: The Stepping Stone's Formula™
Book: Kidz That Dream Big: Dreams Do Come True
https://www.amazon.co.uk/dp/1912547066/ref=cm _sw_r_cp_api_mwbUAbS8BTQHE
Facebook page: Kidz That Dream Big:
https://www.facebook.com/Kidz-that-Dream-BIG-154694734627138/

65

AS SEEN OF TV, RADIO & NEWSPAPERS

Yasmine Ben Salmi is not your average 11yr old. Yasmine Ben Salmi aka LovePreneur is an 11yr award winning author of The Choice is Your - 10 Keys Principles To Create A Happier Lifestyle, Winner of TruLittle Heros Award - Creative 2017, Guest Speaker at The Beat You Expo, Former International Radio Show Host, Member of Team Trouble (participated in campaigns for Sainsburys, Legoland, Warner Bros, Sony and Made For Mums to name a few) founded by Amazing Arabella & JD The Super Car Kid, Yasmine's signature program: Your Thinking C.A.P For Living & Loving Life™, Yasmine's Dog Walking Service "Woof-Woof your dog is here", Nominated for a R.E.E.B.A Award 2017, Winner of Radio Works Authors Awards 2017, Nominated for National Diversity Award 2017, founder of Mum and Daughter Connect Collection and founder of Lovepreneur.
Book: The Choice Is Yours: 10 Key Principles to Create a Happier Lifestyle
https://www.amazon.co.uk/dp/1912547082/ref=cm _sw_r_cp_api_JbaUAbR7K3MNS
Facebook page: Lovepreneur:
https://m.facebook.com/YasmineBenSalmiakaLov ePrenur/

AS SEEN OF TV, RADIO & NEWSPAPERS

9yr old Paolo Ben Salmi aka Pint Size Adventurer is not is not your average 9yr old. Paolo is Water-to-Go's youngest ever ambassador! https://www.watertogo.eu/paolobensalmi blog about Water-to-Go and Paolo: https://www.watertogo.eu/blog/meet-paolo-water-to-gos-youngest-ever-ambassador/ Paolo Ben Salmi is an award winning author of Pint Size Adventurer - 10 Keys Principles To Get Your KIDS off their iPads & Into The Wild.

Award Winning Public Speaker (who has spoken at eleventh such as Mercedes Benz World), Former member of Team Trouble (participated in campaigns for Sainsburys, Legoland, Warner Bros, Sony and Made For Mums to name a few) founded by Amazing Arabella & JD The Super Car Kid, Paolo's signature program is called The Abundant Adventure Inventor™, 2nd place in TruLittle Heros Award - U12 Entrepreneur 2017.

Guest Speaker at The Beat You Expo, Mercedes Benz World 10th April, Official Judge for Made for Mums Toy Awards 2018 via Team Trouble, Former International Radio Show host, 229/17

Paolo made history by being the youngest to interview Dr John Demartini: https://www.facebook.com/350400542063654/videos/363072487463126/ personal developments coach and founder of Pint Size Adventurer who is here to help you to plant the seed toward self-discovery, exploration of the internal and external world and adventurer in abundance via a variety of products and services to assist you to create a brighter future

Book: Pint Size Adventurer: 10 Key Principles to Get Your KIDS off Their iPads & Into the Wild
https://www.amazon.co.uk/dp/1912547031/ref=cm_sw_r_cp_api_iwXXAbMZRM7QA
Facebook page: Pint Size Adventurer:
https://m.facebook.com/paolobensalmiakapintsizeadventurer/

AS SEEN OF TV, RADIO & NEWSPAPERS

Amire Ben Salmi is not your average 5yr old. Amire Ben Salmi aka Mr. Intelligent is a 5yr old award winning author of Because I AM Intelligent - 365 Affirmations To Brighten Up Your Day, Guest Speaker at The Beat You Expo, Member of Team Trouble (participated in campaigns for Sainsburys, Legoland, Warner Bros and Sony to name a few) founded by Amazing Arabella & JD The Super Car Kid, Amire's signature program is Easy-As-P.I.E Affirmatios™ and He's founder of Because I AM Intelligent who is here to help you to plant the seed toward having fun learning during childhood, Positive Affirmations, Fun and Creativity in abundance via a variety of products such as a book with a matching colour car and 52 affirmation cards to assist you to create a brighter future
Book: Because I AM Intelligent 365 Affirmations to Brighten Up Your Day
https://www.amazon.co.uk/dp/1912547023/ref=cm_sw_r_cp_api_gcaUAb6A5W5SJ
Facebook page: Because I AM Intelligent:
https://m.facebook.com/BecauseIAMIntelligent/

SURPRISE BONUS

There comes a time in life when one grows to realise that they merely need to get out of their own way.

You need to just be honest with yourself so you can grow, after all no one is perfect and everyone makes mistakes.

What could you do differently today as a result of the mistakes and lessons that you learned from yesterday?

Who do you need to forgive?

Who do you need to be grateful for?

What action should you take?

Who could you speak to if you need some help?

The moment that you learn how to shift your mindset and get out of your own way is the moment that you will be able to live a truly remarkable life experience.

Become a weed in life, weeds refuse to die... Come rain or shine, through the storms and the snow. No matter what - they are determined to live and grow in any given environment. At times they may be small, nonetheless they are mighty in their determination. The term **"weed"** in its general sense is a subjective one, without any classification value since a **"weed"** is not a weed when growing where it belongs or is wanted. Therefore, I urge you to pursue **your dreams** and surround yourself with people who you like and trust. Plant your roots in fertile soil filled with oceans of love and positivity which will empower and inspire you to thrive and accomplish your desired outcomes.

Just know that change is happening on an unconscious level; therefore, your reality is changing **now**. If you attempt to resist uncomfortable emotions remember - they won't go away. I believe that it's better to express than to repress, otherwise you'll simply increase the negative energy wishing it'd go away. Dwelling upon how unpleasant it makes you feel or worry that it'll get worse - will simply distract your thinking.

Go ahead and simply state how you desire to feel; this has a strange phenomenon of diminishing the unwanted emotions **Are You Ready To TRANSFORM? Yes or No?**
Now! I want you to focus on and fully experience your emotions. This might seem a little odd; and let me just say that being open minded is a good idea right **now.** It will serve you best to face your uncomfortable emotions. The questions which I would like you to fully consider **now** are:

- What do you find uncomfortable about this emotion?
- Is it really so terrible that you can't confront it **now**?
- What would need to happen, in order for you to confront your uncomfortable emotions?
- How do you know?
-

If you can confront your emotions **now**... please go ahead and do so. Just k**now** that it's okay to experience your uncomfortable emotion **now**, in order to best serve you for the next phase in your life journey.

That's right..... Just relax and fully experience your emotions.

If you feel like crying - do so. If you feel like expressing yourself through writing - do so. If you feel like shouting - do so and if you feel like talking - do so. Simply allow your emotions to flow - Whatever it may be for... **JUST DO IT!** Go ahead; it is okay to release energy **now**.

WELL DONE!!! I ADMIRE YOUR COURAGE **Now** - take a deep breath... the fact that you are reading this book means that you are ready to make these changes **now**. So just go ahead and preserve the positive learnings for yourself and for the future. I truly believe that things happen either as a result of something we do - or something we don't do in our lives. As I feel that all problems are problems of the mind, therefore all solutions are also solutions of the mind. You are solely responsible for yourself and cannot control others. However, you are responsible for the way in which you choose to respond or react to the experiences which you encounter within your life journey. In spite of everything, the universe doesn't make mistakes and I totally believe that everything happens for a reason.

Bear in mind - a problem well stated is a problem half solved... Are You Ready To TRANSFORM? **Yes or No?** - I want you to think of a problem and fully consider each of the following questions:
- What is the problem?
- What is the root cause of the problem?
- How have you failed to resolve this?
- How can you overcome this problem?

- What would you like to transform **now**?
- When will you stop it from being a limitation?
- How many ways do you **know** you have solved this?
- How are you changing and seeing things differently **now**?
- How do you **know**?

That was a terrible problem wasn't it? **Now** that you are seeing and understanding things differently, it feels great...
Right! **Yes or No?**
Rest assure as you are exactly where you need to be right **now**..... Preserve the positive *learnings for yourself and the future.

Let's face it! It is your responsibility to gain positive learnings. Look at it this way, one may lead a horse to the water but one can't make the horse drink unless the horse is willing. Do you agree?

It is extremely common for people to feel the need to date immediately after the end of a relationship to avoid feeling invalidated and unloved. This is often in effort to fill the void which was created as a result of their relationship breakdown. I advise that you refrain from dating following a breakup, even if your former partner is dating. I am here to simply remind you that you are the master of your mind... Consequently, you are in control. After all you are putting in place the building blocks for the life you and your dependants deserve, aren't you? **Yes or No?**...

Therefore, I urge you to simply look at this point in your life as an adventure.

After all this is a perfect opportunity for you to explore who you really are? That's right... a precious opportunity to rediscover yourself and your true passions, values and beliefs and so much more.

The questions which I would like you to fully consider **now** are:

-   Who are you? I don't mean... a mother, father, nurse or cashier etc. I mean who are

78

you? After all you are a divine child of God aren't you? And you are the answer to many prays – right? Yes or No?

- Who do you want to be?
- What do you really want in all areas of your life?

I am confidence that these questions will serve you well.

I can appreciate that after years of being in a relationship and defining yourself as a 'wife/husband', 'mother/father' or 'the other half".

You may have lost sight of who you truly are and what you truly desire.

If for any reason you're harbouring a fantasy of the perfect partner or believing that a new relationship will rescue you from whatever you dislike about yourself or your life.

The question which I would like you to fully consider **now** is:
- To what extent are you expecting a relationship to enrich your life?

Okay!... **Now** I suggest that you simply start by working on those things **right now!**

Ultimately when you are satisfied, confident and happy - it is at that precise moment that you can go onto experience true love, happiness, fulfilment, wealth, health and spiritual growth. Bear in mind everything is energy and you'll draw your composite to you, one that will compliment who you truly are.

At times in life you may fall along the way!
-    What do you do when you fall down?

Yes, that's right! **Get back up**... In life there are times when

you may feel like you don't have the strength to **get back up**...

It may even feel impossible to **get back up**...
-    If you don't try will you get up?

No... If you start walking whilst lying flat on your face
-    Will you get anywhere?

No... I urge you to **get back up** right here and right **now**. You must keep trying, because you will learn along the way and more importantly your dependants are always observing you... So take a moment to think about them.

From this day forth if you fall 99 times - you must **get back up** 100 times, because it doesn't matter how many times you fall. What matters most is getting back up and preserving the positive learnings for yourself and for the future and rising up empowered.

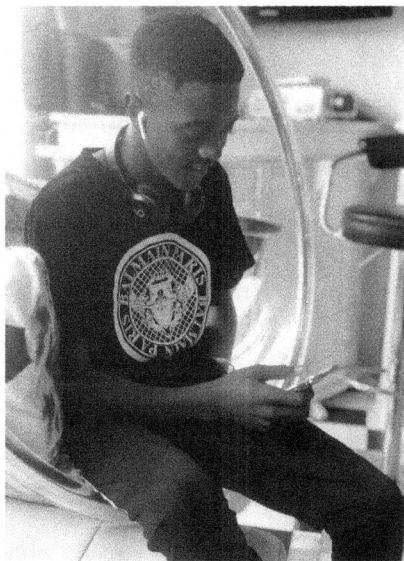

I HOPE THAT THESE PHOTOS INSPIRE YOU TO START YOUR OWN JOURNEY

DISCLAIMER

Tray-Sean Ben Salmi (the authors) are business and life coaches and mentors. Nothing more and nothing less. The Authors cannot, and do not, make any promises, guarantees, warrantees or representations about results other than the coaches diligent work with you. Advices are being provided "AS IS" without warranty of any kind, either express or implied, including without limitation any warranty for information, coaching, products or services provided through or in connection with this book. The advices in this book are requested at the coaching/mentoring participant's own choice and with inherent singular responsibility of the coaching/mentoring participant. The authors would like to explicitly point out that the advices that the author offer do not replace the expertise of a medical doctor or of an alternative non-medicine practitioner. Advices differ decidedly from those of a medical doctor or that of a practitioner in the non-medical area.

The authors do not claim to make any diagnosis or give any promises of any sort of healing processes. The authors are neither qualified nor equipped to deal with a person with pathological history, should you be in medical or psychiatric treatment due to any health issues, it is strongly advised to continue your therapy with your doctors. In case you still want to be coached/mentored by the authors of this book, kindly consult your doctors before contacting the authors. Whatever your decision, please do not interrupt your treatment with your doctor(s).

This book is focused on offering you a host of inspiration and resources to give you a chance to open your mind to the wonders of abundance in life for a more satisfying existence. This book will help you to learn how to loosen the control mechanisms that habitually stop us. For all other physical or mental health issues you are advised to consult professionals who are specifically trained to treat such challenges.

The author shall not be responsible for any loss or damage caused, or alleged to have been caused, directly or indirectly, by the information or ideas contained, suggested, or referenced in this book. However, if any legal relations arise in connection with this book, shall be governed by and construed in accordance with the laws of United Kingdom.

www.ingramcontent.com/pod-product-compliance
Lightning Source LLC
LaVergne TN
LVHW021539080426
835509LV00019B/2737